Innovative Teams

2O MINUTE MANAGER SERIES

Get up to speed fast on essential business skills. Whether you're looking for a crash course or a brief refresher, you'll find just what you need in HBR's 20-Minute Manager series—foundational reading for ambitious professionals and aspiring executives. Each book is a concise, practical primer, so you'll have time to brush up on a variety of key management topics.

Advice you can quickly read and apply, from the most trusted source in business.

Titles include:

Creating Business Plans

Delegating Work

Finance Basics

Getting Work Done

Giving Effective Feedback

Innovative Teams

Managing Projects

Managing Time

Managing Up

Performance Reviews

Presentations

Running Meetings

2O MINUTE MANAGER SERIES

Innovative Teams

Unlock creative energy
Generate new ideas
Brainstorm effectively

HARVARD BUSINESS REVIEW PRESS

Boston, Massachusetts

Portions of this work, including core concepts, are derived from the book *When Sparks Fly: Igniting Creativity in Groups* by Dorothy Leonard and Walter Swap (Harvard Business School Publishing, 1999).

The web addresses referenced in this book were live and correct at the time of the book's publication but may be subject to change.

Library of Congress Cataloging-in-Publishing Data

Innovative teams : unlock creative energy, generate new ideas, brainstorm effectively.
    pages cm.—(20 minute manager series)
  Includes index.
  ISBN 978-1-63369-004-2
  1. Creative ability in business.   2. Creative thinking.   3. New products.   4. Teams in the workplace—Management.   I. Harvard Business Review Press.
  HD53.I5645 2015
  658.4′022—dc23

                                                            2014044998
ISBN: 9781633690042
eISBN: 9781633690059   5660 2799   05/15

Preview

You have a problem: Perhaps your company needs a new service to offer its customers or an internal process is taking too long. Your usual solutions aren't working, so you need something different, something creative. Innovative thinking can help you and your team meet urgent needs or make small but important improvements. This book walks you through each step of the creative process. You'll learn to:

- Build the diversity of your team to maximize creative potential

- Establish the right time and setting for idea generation

- Set ground rules for team interactions

- Draw on a variety of approaches to crafting ideas

- Narrow down your options to a useful solution

- Instill a culture of creativity within your organization

Contents

Contents

Innovative Teams

Enhancing Your Team's Creativity

Enhancing Your Team's Creativity

D o you need to create a new, innovative product? Is your organization looking for a unique plan for entering into new international markets? Or do you need to think differently about how to break down silos between departments within your organization? All of these tasks require your team to be creative.

But how do you generate ideas—the right ideas—if your team is just going through the motions and stuck in a rut? Fortunately, you can take concrete steps to stimulate your group's creative energy. By understanding the fundamentals of the creative process as well as the characteristics of creative teams, you can lead your team to more-innovative thinking—and to new products, better problem solving, improved processes, superior strategic plans, and more.

What is creativity?

Creativity is the ability to develop novel ideas to solve problems or satisfy needs. It's a key ingredient in *innovation*, which generally refers to that novel idea along with its practical application. An innovative team, as we'll discuss in this book, is a group of individuals who envision and develop creative solutions to problems.

Enhancing team creativity is a goal-oriented, collaborative process that draws on each individual team member's skills, experience, and expertise to develop those novel ideas. This kind of thinking isn't reserved for just the "creatives" in your organization. Whether you're leading artists or accountants, a group of 12 in a nonprofit or a team of 12,000 in a *Fortune* 500 company, everyone involved can contribute.

Situations that call for creativity

Many common product-development challenges can best be tackled with innovative thinking. For example, maybe you're in charge of designing a new product line. The last line was a flop, so the pressure's on to create new products that wow. Or maybe you've recently launched a web-based service that your customers love. They're hungry for an app to complement the service—but how should it work? Or imagine that your competitor has released a much-heralded new product. What can your organization do to maintain market share? Creativity can help your company stand out, design products that provide a better user experience, devise new ways to engage your customers, develop interesting ways to market a product, and build your competitive advantage.

You can also harness your team's inventive thinking to solve problems that may not directly affect your customers but have an adverse impact on your organization's effectiveness. Maybe an internal process is cumbersome and time-consuming: The invoicing process is overly complex, or a certain report is always submitted late, no matter who's writing it. A creative team can identify better ways to execute the process at hand. Perhaps you're unsure how to communicate a new initiative in a way that will both excite and involve your colleagues. Wherever you need new solutions or ideas, the creative process can help.

Not every problem requires a novel solution, however. The creative process may not be right for you if:

- Your team is short-handed, dealing with an urgent problem, or rushing to meet a deadline.

In such cases, the creative process can be a distraction (or a procrastination strategy) that will only slow you down. Aim for the most efficient solution, not the most innovative one.

- You have a client who is content with what you're providing and is risk-averse or dislikes change. Your client will likely be happiest with the status quo; don't rock the boat.

- You don't have the resources—whether talent, time, or money—to implement a new idea. Coming up with creative ideas without a realistic way to execute them can be a waste of time, and it is frustrating for a team to expend its creative energy on something that won't come to fruition.

- Major change is imminent in your organization—be it a merger, acquisition, or reorganization. Investing your time in a creative solution that could become irrelevant in the new version of your organization may be unproductive. Wait. You'll soon encounter a new set of problems to solve creatively.

Benefits of the creative process

We've looked at some of the benefits of using the creative process in situations from product development to internal process improvement. But fostering creativity in your team doesn't just help you solve the problem at hand. By making your team aware of creative possibilities, you can discover new information and hidden needs, which can lead you toward even better products, improved processes, and more.

Fostering creativity is also central to engagement: When an employee helps craft a creative solution to a problem, he's more likely to feel a sense of ownership—and may be more motivated to ensure a project's success.

What this book will do

This book will walk you through each step of leading the creative process within your team, no matter what challenge you're facing. These steps include:

- Establishing a team with the right blend of intellectual diversity

- Setting the right time and place for creative thinking and establishing group norms

- Generating a wide array of ideas using various techniques, including brainstorming as well as some less familiar tactics

- Narrowing down your options and using the right criteria to decide which idea to pursue and how

You'll also learn how to promote ongoing creativity in your team and organization by building a culture that embraces and rewards inventive thinking and innovative efforts.

Your opportunity to adapt a fresh, new way of thinking starts now. In the next chapter, we'll tackle the first step of the process: building your innovative team.

Building
Your Team

Building Your Team

B efore you can boost your team's creativity, you should first make sure your team is poised for success. Do you have the right team members in place with the skills, backgrounds, and expertise to generate and refine great ideas?

This chapter will explain what your creative team should look like, show you how to assess where your team needs improvement, and help you enhance the group's potential by bringing in new members or providing opportunities for individual employees' development.

The characteristics of innovative teams

Inventive thinking in a team setting is fueled by a blend of talents, skills, and traits—such as an ability to see problems through fresh eyes, a knack for understanding a frustrated customer's complaints, or a flair for turning a creative idea into a profitable innovation—that rarely exist in a single person. This kind of diversity is more likely to be present when individuals on the team come from different disciplines, backgrounds, and areas of expertise. A choir can't perform well if it's made up of all sopranos; similarly, on an innovative team, you won't achieve good results with people whose strengths and styles are all the same.

The most productive creative teams often exhibit characteristics that seem contradictory. For example, a group needs both expertise in relevant subjects and fresh eyes that can see beyond the established ways of doing things. Its members need the freedom to decide how to achieve goals while also having the discipline to work in alignment with the organization's strategy. An innovative team needs to be both playful and professional, and it needs to be able to plan out a project carefully while also accepting that projects don't always go as planned—and being willing to improvise when unexpected events arise.

To build a team that, as a whole, can navigate effectively among these different dynamics, you need to shape your group so that each individual brings a unique combination of knowledge and skills. You may need people with relevant experience within a specific industry, the ability to perform a particular technical skill, or a talent for writing or presentation. You'll also want team members who excel in interpersonal dynamics such as building consensus, giving feedback, communicating in groups, and motivating others.

In addition to recruiting team members with a mix of skills and experience, you'll want to include individuals with a blend of different preferred thinking styles, or unconscious ways of looking at and interacting with the world. There are many different ways to describe how people think. The Myers-Briggs Type Indicator, for example, divides thinking preferences into four categories:

- *Extroverted or introverted.* Extroverts look to other people as their primary means of processing information. They quickly share ideas or problems with others for feedback. Introverts tend to process information internally before presenting their results to others.

- *Sensing or intuitive.* Sensing people prefer using facts and hard data to help them make decisions. Intuitive people tend to be more comfortable with "big picture" ideas and concepts.

- *Thinking or feeling.* Thinking people use logic and order to make their decisions. Feeling people are more attuned to emotional cues; their decisions are guided by the values or relationships involved.

- *Judging or perceiving.* People who judge prefer having closure, with all loose ends tied up, when managing tasks and making decisions. Those who perceive are more comfortable with openness and ambiguity. They often want to gather more data before making a final decision.

Everyone exhibits all eight of these qualities in varying degrees, though we do have innate preferences. For example, a feeling person is not incapable of logical thought, nor is intuition absent in a sensing person. But a feeling person is more likely to respond emotionally to a problem before applying a logical lens, and a sensing person may prefer to make a decision based on hard data rather than on a theory. Preferences can also change in different contexts. You may have a tendency toward perception when visiting your child's classroom but employ judgment when at jury duty.

No one style is better than another, and each carries its own set of benefits to a collaborative discussion. The ideas and solutions that an intellectually diverse team generates will be richer and more valuable due to the wide variety of perspectives that inform them. Diversity of thought and perspective can protect your team from groupthink and can spark *creative abrasion*, a process in which potential solutions are generated, explored, and altered through debate and discourse.

Assess your team

Now that you understand what an innovative team looks like, think about your own group. If you've inherited an existing team or are newly embarking on the creative process with a group you already manage, take this opportunity to get to know each individual, assessing her skills and other elements of intellectual diversity. (If you are starting a new group, see the sidebar "Building a team from scratch.")

The best way to get to know your team and assess its range of skills and experience is through conversation. It can be helpful to do this as a group, so everyone can learn what each team member brings to the table. Ask each person a few directed questions:

- What's your work history, both at this company and in previous jobs?

- What's your educational background? What did you study in college or for an advanced degree?

- What strengths do you have, and what do others say you do well?

- What are your passions and hobbies?

You may already know the answers to some of these questions, based on your prior experience with these individuals. But many of us have interests and experiences unrelated to our jobs. Tapping into these areas at work can kindle passion and introduce ingenuity. The sales manager who is interested in art history may be your best big-picture thinker. The sound engineer who used to work as a stage director might bring expertise to the management of the creative process. And the marathon runner can bring grit and commitment to your team, motivating others when times get tough.

Also ask about prior team experiences, which will allow you and the rest of the team to learn about people's preferred work styles and different ways of thinking. For example:

- What was your best team experience? Why? What did team members or the leader do to make it a good experience?

- What was your worst team experience? Why? What behaviors made you frustrated or uncomfortable?

- What do you like most about working on a team, and what do you struggle with?

- How do you define a good teammate, team leader, and meeting?

- What do you need from a team to do your best work?

You may not be able to meet every request or preference discussed, but understanding team members' strengths and proclivities will help you bring out the group's inventiveness as you progress through the creative process.

Seek new members

Now that you've gotten to know your team, consider what's missing. Are there any relevant skills or areas of expertise that you don't have covered? Maybe

BUILDING A TEAM FROM SCRATCH

There may be an instance where you have the opportunity for a creative venture, but you have no existing team in place to work on it. In such cases, you have the opportunity to build your team from scratch.

To begin, assess your needs. When staffing a creative team, first envision the results you want, and then determine what skills and capabilities you'll need to achieve them. (If you want to build a mobile app, for example, you'll need expertise in technology, development, and user experience at the very least.) Once you have an individual on board with a particular critical skill, move on to the next person you'll require. You

you've assembled a group of big-picture thinkers who can generate lots of potential solutions to a problem, but you're missing a detail-oriented planner who will focus on how to execute on those ideas and help keep the project grounded. Or maybe you have plenty of don't need more than one person with the same area of expertise.

Pick people who differ from you in thinking style and experience. As we've already discussed, a team that is made up of mixed approaches and areas of expertise will do better work than a group of too-similar people.

Your team should be high in diversity and low in number. Select the fewest people who can help you achieve the results you want. Three to seven people is ideal. The more individuals you have involved, the more difficult it will be to schedule meetings, manage information, and make decisions.

marketing know-how but lack someone well versed in accounting or design who can bring your project to fruition. If you discover gaps, consider who else you can bring onto your team. Depending on the scale of your project, you may want to look outside your department, company, or even industry to find the expertise you need.

Before you start hunting, define your criteria. Create a job description that's specific to the type of person (or people) you need, clearly identifying the skills and areas of expertise required

Then, look within your organization for people on other teams or in other departments with the skills or background you're searching for. Ask colleagues if they can recommend someone. For bigger projects, perhaps some of your overseas colleagues can visit and temporarily join your team. Or former employees can return, bringing along knowledge they've gleaned by working at other organizations.

Talk to promising candidates—and their supervisors—about becoming part of your team. Do they have the time and resources to join you as a full-on team member? If not, consider building a support team that you can consult with periodically throughout the creative process to complement your core team. For example, just because you may want to invite a finance representative to weigh in on your budget request doesn't mean that person needs to participate in your idea generation session.

If individuals within your company can't fill your gaps, go outside your organization—or even outside your industry. For instance, when engineers working at a ceramics manufacturer were having difficulty getting the ceramics to release from their molds, they realized that their problem had to do with quick freezing, not with ceramics. Instead of seeking out other ceramics experts, they turned to experts in the food industry who would have more experience with this process. You can do the same thing by asking those in your network for referrals, or by asking friends outside your industry to be on the lookout for the expertise you need. Consider recruiting individuals who may be able to take on part-time roles or internships, like professors on sabbaticals, students, and others who are making job transitions. You might also meet a suitable candidate at a conference or industry event, or even on job websites or social media platforms such as LinkedIn.

Once you've found someone of interest, bring her in for a formal interview so you can get to know her, much like you did for the rest of your team. This is especially important if it's for a bigger creative venture. Résumés and cover letters will likely reveal the applicant's education and work background, so instead spend your time trying to understand what the candidate would bring to the table in terms of her thinking style, interests, experience, and interpersonal behaviors. For smaller projects or if you're pressed for time, a short, informal conversation may be enough to determine whether a candidate will fit your needs.

Once you've found your new team members, carefully and deliberately integrate them into the group. Otherwise, these new arrivals could feel isolated or become marginalized. Here are some ways to ensure that your new teammates are comfortable with their new group:

- Thoughtfully prepare your group for any upcoming additions. Discuss in advance why it's valuable to include people with different perspectives and skills, and ensure that the new members' roles within the team are clear to everyone.

- Match newcomers with seasoned mentors to help them acclimate to the team quickly, and ensure that new team members understand how the existing team works.

- Make meaningful introductions. Existing team members may already know one another's skills, interests, and styles, but sharing that information with new members can help both veterans and newcomers bond.

- Finally, meet early on with new team members to discuss their experience with the group and address any difficulties.

Enhance creative potential on an existing team

In some cases, you may not have the opportunity to bring on new members. You can still develop the diversity of your existing team's skills by:

- *Building expertise.* Send your people to professional conferences, or arrange training sessions to help them gain the skills and better understanding of processes. New knowledge can catalyze your team's creative thinking.

- *Taking field trips.* Arrange a site visit to a customer or even to a competitor. Or observe best practices in an unfamiliar industry. For example, an airline hoping to improve customer service might visit a clothing retailer known for its excellence in that area.

- *Hosting creative events.* Bring in outside speakers to give talks or workshops. One automaker runs periodic events where employees can meet different types of artists—sculptors, DJs, chefs, photographers, writers—to learn about their creative processes.

- *Seeking additional resources.* Gather your team to watch and discuss a TED talk (popcorn optional), or form an ad hoc reading club to discuss books or articles of interest.

By building a team with a diverse set of skills, experience, and thinking styles, you'll be ready to infuse a variety of perspectives and opinions into a creative conversation. Once you have your team in place, your next step is to construct the right environment for creative thinking.

Setting the Stage for Creative Thinking

Setting the Stage for Creative Thinking

After you have your team in place, you're ready to start thinking inventively with them, right? Wrong. First you need to prepare. Where should your idea generation session take place? What information do you need in advance? How should your team members interact with one another? This chapter will help you determine the best time for idea generation, secure the right physical space, and set team ground rules before you dive into creative thinking.

Find the right time

Plan the timing for your idea generation session carefully. Imagining ideas, winnowing down options, and crafting a plan to move forward typically can't be completed in one meeting, so before you set a meeting time, create an overarching timeline. When do you need your fresh idea to come to fruition? Once you've identified a deadline, work back from there to decide when the best time for idea generation would be, remembering to reserve time in the schedule afterward for consideration and implementation of ideas.

When in doubt, plan your idea generation session far in advance of your deadline. Many people assume that creative minds come up with their best ideas when time is tight—but that's rarely true. Allowing too little time for the idea generation process due to an unnecessarily restrictive deadline can short circuit your efforts and hamper innovation. Teams that are pushed to work creatively within an arbitrarily short time frame can end up frustrated and burned out. Of course, some instances may require an urgent solution. If your team is under extreme time constraints, see the sidebar "Time pressure."

Once you've determined how much time you have, schedule a meeting to generate ideas. Creative sessions can be mentally demanding, so reserve about 30 minutes for your session. An hour-long meeting (or more) can be exhausting, and you'll soon discover that you had your best ideas earlier in the meeting. If you decide that your team needs more time, you can always reconvene, but it's better to stop and schedule a follow-up meeting than to force your group to keep grinding away unproductively.

Some times of day are more conducive to creativity than others. Morning sessions can be more productive than afternoon sessions, when people are tired and energy flags—although you should refrain from scheduling meetings first thing in the morning, when people are still settling into the workday.

Avoid times when your team may be too distracted to dedicate their time and energy to creative efforts. If your team is dealing with an urgent project unrelated to your creative task, find another time to meet when you can have the group's full attention. On the day before a holiday or long weekend—even on a regular Friday afternoon—people will be rushing to check off everything on their to-do lists, and you won't be able to keep their focus. Similarly, the day before or after a team member's vacation is not ideal. In either case he'll likely be bogged down with other tasks.

Set the scene

Choosing a meeting location with a dull atmosphere can stifle an inventive discussion. When an environment provides different kinds of stimuli, on the other

TIME PRESSURE

Ingenuity can flourish under extreme time pressure. One well-known example: the NASA team that dropped everything and, within hours, came up with an inelegant but effective fix for the failing air-filtration system on Apollo 13—a creative solution that saved the mission and crew. But don't be fooled into thinking that time pressure on its own will spur creativity.

Creative thinking is certainly possible under high, even extreme, time pressure, but only when people are able to be deeply immersed in the urgent problem. If you are forced to accelerate the creative process:

- *Explain the urgency.* When people understand that their work is critical, they become more involved and feel positively challenged. Let them know why their work is important and needed

(*continued*)

TIME PRESSURE

so fast, so they don't feel they're being pushed to meet an arbitrary deadline.

- *Help them focus.* People do better creative work when they're able to concentrate on a single activity without interruption. Protect your creative team from distractions and unrelated demands by freeing them from less-essential tasks and meetings.

- *Work in small groups.* Under time pressure, collaboration is more effective when it's concentrated. Have your team work in small groups or even in pairs. The entire team can then reconvene to discuss their findings, if that will help advance the project.

While these tactics can be effective, unnecessary deadlines and time constraints can still cause more harm than good when it comes to creativity. But by approaching the situation with a clear purpose and by positioning your team to work effectively, you can help your team members become invested and accepting of time pressure, giving way to more collaborative and creative results.

hand, it encourages team members to make new connections and think more broadly—and it sends an outward signal that this meeting will require different thinking.

If possible, choose a location where your team rarely meets: The same old conference room can feel stale and uninviting. If you need to meet in your usual space, play around with the room setup. Instead of sitting around a conference table, position chairs in clusters. Or, if the tables are usually set up in small groups, push them all together to make one large table or circle. Select seating that will encourage activity and collaboration. That cozy armchair may not motivate someone to leap up and draw on the board, but an upright posture—on backless stools or even standing—encourages people to stay alert and engaged.

Provide warm light to create an energizing environment. Open the blinds or provide floor lamps to combat the draining quality of overhead fluorescents. And if it fits your organizational culture, perk people up by playing background music.

Ask your team to leave all laptops, tablets, phones, and other devices behind. Instead, supply the room with tactile tools beyond the traditional whiteboard: huge pieces of paper, small colorful sticky notes, or a blackboard with colorful chalk. Cover any tables with paper that can be used for note taking, doodling, or drawing, and provide colored pens or pencils, markers, crayons, pipe cleaners, even clay. Art supplies can help bypass inhibition and ignite the imagination.

Do your homework

Gather any existing materials that might be relevant to your problem or situation—including documents, reports, or in-house materials—before your team members convene. Having a clear understanding of what the current situation is will help you imagine possible solutions.

Also seek out existing knowledge about the problem at hand by searching through relevant literature on the web, talking to experts, and investigating the source of the problem. You might do this research yourself or assign specific team members to do it. Experts are almost always happy to talk about what they know best, so it's worth picking up the phone to speak with someone who knows more about a particular problem than you do. (Use the phone here, or even meet in person; you'll learn much more by having a conversation than by exchanging e-mails.) Tap into university, professional, and personal networks to find ways to connect with knowledgeable experts.

Share the findings with the entire team prior to meeting so participants can get a handle on the problem, and route any relevant materials to team members early so they can read them in advance.

Finally, communicate a clear agenda before the meeting. People need to know before they convene if they'll be generating ideas or evaluating already existing ones.

Establish rules of conduct

At the start of your idea generation session, establish guidelines for interaction within your team. Your team members need to feel that they won't be humiliated, judged, or punished—by you or anyone else—for speaking up, expressing concerns, suggesting unpopular ideas, or making mistakes. You want a team made up of people who listen to one another, who are open to other viewpoints, and who challenge one another's assumptions—without becoming aggressive.

Establishing rules of the road will help the group identify what's appropriate before potential tension arises—and it's possible that the very process of developing these norms can keep violations in check.

Start with four rules that are appropriate for any creative group:

1. *Respect all members of the group.* Ideas and assumptions may be attacked; individuals may not.

2. *Be a good listener.* Everyone will have an opportunity to speak and should actively listen to others.

3. *Value varying points of view.* Everyone has a right to disagree and challenge assumptions. Conflicting views are a valuable source of

learning and should be welcome when raised at the appropriate time in the discussion.

4. *No idea is a bad idea.* No idea should be deemed "bad," "stupid," "useless," or any other negative descriptor that can shut down creative thinking.

Next, team members can work together to define additional norms based on the unique preferences and working styles of those in the group.

One way to establish these additional rules is to have each person write out a few conditions they feel are essential for doing productive work. You might find, for example, that people's must-haves include starting meetings on time, arriving prepared, and giving notice if you can't attend a meeting. Also ask everyone to write out some things they can't tolerate such as interrupting others, becoming defensive when someone's idea is challenged, or making sarcastic or snide remarks when conveying disagreement.

Discuss these conditions, and gather the team's suggestions into a clear, concise list. Make sure everyone contributes to the discussion. When team members help determine the rules of behavior, they feel a sense of ownership of the guidelines as well as a sense of team identity. Once you've finalized the list, keep it handy so that your team can refer to it, particularly if any issues arise.

With rules of interaction in place, you can now move on to generating creative ideas.

Generating Ideas

Generating Ideas

Creative ideas arise from *divergent thinking*, in which you and your team break away from familiar or established ways of seeing and doing things to come up with something new and fresh. This type of thinking allows your team to see from different perspectives, discover new connections among facts or events, and explore questions that have never been asked before.

The goal of divergent thinking is to quickly generate a wide variety of solutions for a given situation or problem without judging the merits of those options. In this step of the process, you don't yet narrow down the options that you create. Creating and winnowing down your options at the same time is like driving with your foot on the brake: You'll expend a lot of energy but get nowhere.

This chapter will walk you through how to create novel ideas through the use of four different common creative approaches: brainstorming, mind mapping, catchball, and individual idea generation.

Brainstorming

Brainstorming, probably the most well-known option for divergent thinking, is a method of soliciting ideas from a group quickly. It's especially useful if you want to engage everyone on the team in an informal way. With brainstorming, you can come up with myriad new ideas, understand a problem better by listing possible causes, and solve a problem by gathering a multitude of possible solutions.

Your goal in a brainstorming session should be quantity over quality, and you should encourage even the wildest ideas, no matter how strange, fanciful, or offbeat. Every idea is valuable—you never know where it may lead. Encourage team members to build on one another's ideas, and don't fall into the trap of latching on to the first option your team comes up with. Generate as many ideas as you can. Make sure to have a way to capture all of your ideas, such as a whiteboard or a large sheet of paper.

Have high aspirations for what you'd like your group to achieve. If your team easily comes up with five ideas, push for twenty. Set a stretch goal—even an unreasonable goal—by challenging your team to come up with, say, fifty ideas in three minutes, or a hundred in five minutes. Pushing for more options can send your team off into interesting new directions. People will inevitably throw out some ideas that are duds—but don't judge. As the list of ideas grows and people feel pressured to come up with more, their thinking will become more inventive.

Use these four brainstorming techniques to get your team's creative juices flowing:

1. *Exploring.* Use guided imagery—symbols, analogies, and metaphors—to generate options. For instance, if your group is trying to create a new, truly innovative customer service initiative, you could say, "What are the feelings that you want your ideal level of service to generate in customers?" Or, "Draw an image that symbolizes what you think of as best-practice service." Use these attributes and illustrations to come up with potential solutions to your problem—a new ratings system that incorporates those feelings of satisfaction and happiness or a customer engagement event with employees that can achieve a level of personal connection to create that smiley-face picture your team member drew.

2. *Visioning.* Ask group members to imagine an ideal solution in great detail and then identify what the means for achieving it might

be. For example, "If our consulting company could provide *any* services, what would they be?" Ignore constraints; be impractical. If money, time, and resources were no object, what ideas would produce the ideal future? Push even further by asking team members to imagine themselves five to seven years into the future. What would the situation look like then? What would the team have accomplished? The goal of this technique is to break free of the practicality that can inhibit creative thought. After this imaginative process, follow up with information gathering and analysis to identify what it would take to make these ideal solutions happen.

3. *Modifying.* While visioning entails imagining a future world with no constraints, modifying asks you to consider the current situation and change or adapt it. For instance, let's say

your team needs to reduce the number of errors when entering customer information into a company database. Look at the situation through the eyes of those who use the program. What would you adapt to make this software more intuitive? What features or functionality could be added to double-check the data?

4. *Experimenting.* Systematically combine elements, test the combinations, and see if they reveal valuable new ideas. You can express this visually by creating a matrix with categories across the top row. For example, if a car-washing company were looking to break into a new market, the team might list products washed, equipment, and products sold across the top of the matrix. Then, under each category, list all the possible variations you can think of—even if they seem outrageous. For

example, equipment variations might include sprays, conveyors, stalls, and brushes; products washed might include cars, boats, and dogs. (See table 1, "Car wash experimenting matrix.")

The resulting table allows the team to put together new business possibilities by combining the options listed in each column: selling microfiber cleaning cloths to motorcycle owners, starting a service for boaters to wash their boats using stalls, sprayers, and conveyors—or, as a stretch option, power-washing homes using sprays and hoses.

Throughout your session—no matter which of the four brainstorming techniques you choose—move at a fast clip; if the conversation slows, people may start to censor themselves. If the process stalls and no one is suggesting an idea, restate the problem in a different way or ask a new question to prompt more suggestions.

TABLE 1

Car wash experimenting matrix

Products washed	Equipment	Products sold
Cars	Sprays	Upholstery shampoo
Motorcycles	Conveyors	Travel-size trash bags
Construction equipment	Stalls	Microfiber cloths
Lawn mowers	Dryers	Car fragrance spray
Houses	Brushes	Hanging car air fresheners
Clothes	Hoses	Gift cards
Boats		Squeegees
Upholstered furniture		Windshield wiper blades
Horses		Windshield washer fluid
Dogs		

You can also combine your brainstorming efforts with physical activity. For example, have your team members write ideas on a paper airplane and toss it to another person. As each person catches the plane, they can write down a new idea. The physical stimulation and freedom of play can bring about new ideas.

Mind mapping

Brainstorming can give a team the opportunity to come up with a long list of options quickly, particularly if there aren't any ideas to start with. Another approach to consider if you're starting with a blank slate is a free association activity called mind mapping. Mind mapping lets you think associatively and visually to develop a constellation of interconnected ideas. Your team may be able to generate more connections between ideas using this format than it would by simply listing ideas.

Begin by writing a keyword or concept relevant to the situation at hand in the center of a blank page or whiteboard. Have your team free associate by adding words that relate to the original concept. Just as in brainstorming, don't evaluate or judge any of the ideas that are put on the map. Even the most outlandish words or phrases can generate fresh thinking.

Connect your ideas by drawing lines between them. Encourage your team to use colors to indicate action items, ideas, doubts, and other important factors. If ideas end up on the board that don't directly connect with a given thought, that's ok. Just leave them on the board for the rest of the team to see. Introduce constraints to challenge your team. For example, try limiting the idea discussion by using only a small page.

You'll end up with a visual mind map—a messy web of related concepts—that looks like figure 1, "Sample mind map." Give the team the opportunity to discuss it, so that everyone can understand each other's viewpoints and contributions.

Catchball

Both mind mapping and brainstorming are great options for a team that needs to start the idea generation process from scratch. If your team already has an

FIGURE 1

Sample mind map

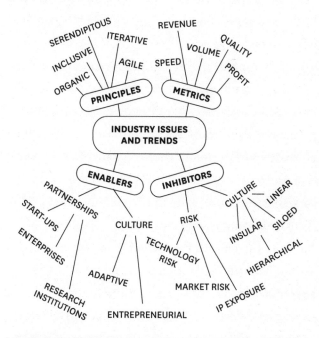

Source: Duarte, Nancy. *HBR Guide to Persuasive Presentations.* Boston: Harvard Business Review Press, 2012.

idea or two to start with (such as an existing product or the typical solution to a common problem), consider using the catchball approach. Catchball has two goals: to improve on an existing idea and to gain buy-in among participants.

In this approach, someone on the team "tosses" the initial idea to someone else. Whoever "catches" the idea must understand it, reflect on it, and improve on it in some way. Then that person tosses the modified idea back to the group, where it's caught by someone else and improved further. (If this approach makes someone freeze up, invite the rest of the team to help.) As each person participates, she will have the opportunity to tinker with the idea and enrich the conversation. This will give each team member a sense of shared responsibility and commitment to the idea—a feeling of ownership that will remain once it's time to implement the idea, no matter who initially introduced it.

Consider the following example. Members of a neighborhood association are concerned about the large number of bike accidents at a certain intersection and want to gather ideas to take to city officials. Jake is the first to get the ball, saying, "The traffic light pattern needs to be changed. Too many cars try to get through the yellow light." He passes the ball to Sonia, who elaborates: "Maybe there needs to be a 'left on green arrow only' signal." Next, to Pierre: "I like that. Can they shorten the yellow light, too?" Finally, to Allison: "And maybe reprogram the traffic light pattern for a few blocks in each direction, so fewer cars end up fighting through that intersection at once." The team now has some ideas to present at the next city council meeting.

As your team builds ideas, assign someone to write down each and every one—no matter how silly—so you can discuss them later. One risk of the catchball approach is that it can push your team to move from generating ideas to narrowing down those options too fast. It's important to separate these two processes, so make it clear to your team that you're focusing on idea generation and nothing else.

Individual idea generation

Some people come up with their best ideas in a collaborative setting, but others will produce more and better ideas working on their own. If your team seems hesitant to jump into a discussion, consider implementing a hybrid structure in which people first work independently and then together. (This hybrid structure can also work well with brainstorming and mind mapping techniques.) Here are three options for the hybrid approach:

1. *Initiate individual discussion.* Ask your team members to silently consider creative solutions to the problem and write down their ideas. They can do this at their desks, in a quiet room, or even around a table in the same room, but be sure to reconvene as a group once everyone is finished. Go around the room and ask each person to read what she's written

down. Make sure everyone gets a chance to speak. If you don't understand an individual's response or you think her idea can be broadened, take the time to ask her to clarify her thinking.

2. *Use sticky notes as visual cues.* Have your team members write down their ideas on sticky notes. Then, have people place them on the wall for all to see. (If your team members would rather remain anonymous, ask one person to gather the notes and place them on the wall.) Invite the group to arrange the ideas in a way that makes sense—perhaps according to a category scheme, a mind map, or something else entirely. Then initiate a conversation with the group to elaborate on the ideas.

3. *Keep it anonymous.* Ask your team members to write down their ideas anonymously and hand them to a designated recorder to read

aloud. Each team member should then rate each idea in order of value from 0 to 10 and hand their ratings to the recorder. That individual then tallies the ratings and posts them for the team to see. The team can then discuss each idea without fear that anyone's ideas or ratings will be judged.

If you don't want your team to go so far as to work alone but you still don't think a large group exercise is a good option, encourage team members to generate ideas with one another in small groups. Break the team into pairs or small clusters to talk, and then reconvene the whole team to share any ideas in a larger discussion. Make sure that at least one person from each group speaks up.

Though brainstorming and other divergent thinking activities are at the heart of the creative process, they're only one step. Next you need to decide which ideas are worth pursuing.

Choosing the Right Option

Choosing the Right Option

D eveloping creative ideas can be exciting, but there's a difference between an intriguing idea and a real business opportunity or viable solution. Moving from many options to a single path forward can be the trickiest part of the creative process. This chapter will help you narrow down the ideas you've generated and create a plan for implementation.

Evaluate useful ideas

It's best to allot some time between your idea generation session and narrowing those ideas down. A few days or even a couple of weeks is ideal, but at a minimum, give your group a night to "sleep on it." This will allow team members to consider their options and think deeply before commenting. During this time, new ideas may emerge, as well as sudden insights about which ideas may be best to pursue.

Once the incubation period has passed, reconvene your team for *convergent thinking*, in which a team shifts its focus from generating novel ideas to considering which of those ideas are useful. The convergent thinking process tempers creativity with discipline, helping you channel the results of idea generation into a new product, service, process improvement, or solution to a problem.

During idea generation, judgment and critical thought were banished. Now it's time to invite those qualities back into the room. At this point in the process, you'll define the constraints you're working with and ask challenging questions to rule out the ideas that don't seem feasible. You'll identify the best ones to pursue and then assess how best to proceed.

It's important to welcome—even encourage—dissent during convergent thinking. Your team should feel free to disagree and express contrary views, as long as that doesn't escalate into unproductive conflict. (See the sidebar "Handling interpersonal conflict" for advice on how to prevent and alleviate this type of tension.) If you find that your team quickly converges into comfortable agreement, don't settle too early: Assign someone to be a devil's advocate to challenge assumptions. An opposing viewpoint can help members reexamine their positions and make a better choice.

Narrow down your list

The work of convergence involves setting limits: narrowing the field of options using a given set of constraints. Once defined, constraints can help you rule out options that are beyond the scope of your project

HANDLING INTERPERSONAL CONFLICT

Despite your best efforts, you may end up with unproductive tension in your team. As important as team diversity and creative abrasion are for imaginative thinking, they can also lead to interpersonal conflict that can be destructive to the entire group. This conflict will only intensify as you delve more deeply into convergent thinking and work pressures mount, so you must deal with it deliberately, thoughtfully, and immediately. Unaddressed, a difficult issue can tamp down your team's energy and hamper its creativity.

If conflict is simmering, first review the group norms with the team. You may have agreed that every team member should have a chance to voice his dissenting opinion, but only ideas—not people—will be judged. Reminding your team of these rules will set the stage for a productive conversation about the issue at hand.

Next, discuss the problem. For example, say you're dealing with someone who is bothered by another team member controlling the discussion. One of your team members, Dawn, might say, "Carlos argues against every idea we propose and controls the conversation. I'm getting frustrated with the project, since it seems like every idea we've suggested doesn't seem viable in his view." Ask Dawn to explain how the behavior affects her with specific examples, making sure that she only speaks for herself. Speaking for others ("Everybody thinks . . .") could cause the person being criticized to become defensive or tune out.

Then, give others in the group the opportunity to discuss the issue so you can fairly assess the root cause of the problem. For example, Carlos may explain that he finds overcoming challenges to be motivating for him, so positing obstacles to each idea is his useful contribution to the group. Others may then admit that

(*continued*)

HANDLING INTERPERSONAL CONFLICT

they are overwhelmed by the sheer number of ideas being discussed and welcome Carlos's attempt to eliminate some options.

Keep the conversation as impersonal as possible, and don't assign blame. After hearing all sides, you may discover that Carlos's behavior is not the problem; instead, different thinking styles and preferences are at play. In that case, perhaps the team could agree that each member can only name one or two obstacles for a particular idea before passing the torch to someone else to share his opinion. That way, Carlos's points will be heard without taking over the entire conversation.

If you discover during the discussion that the subject is too sensitive, tempers are heated, or the meeting is going nowhere, adjourn until a later date so that people can cool down or until you can bring in a facilitator to help keep these interactions more impersonal.

In extreme instances, even after taking these steps, the conflict may be too much for the team to handle. You may need to assess whether asking a team member or two to leave the group would be the best option for the sake of the project.

or are a poor fit for your organization. Consider your company's culture, mission, priorities, and resources, as well as the purpose of your creative project, and evaluate each option your team generated according to these criteria.

These following parameters can help winnow down your options:

- *Organizational values.* Does the idea align with our purpose, mission, and strategy? Does it fit within our culture?

- *Resources.* Can we realistically execute this idea? Do we have the resources—office space, technology, or supplies—available? Do we have the technical and business competencies to make it happen and be successful?

- *Time frame.* What is our time frame for completing the project? Is it doable within that time period?

- *Costs.* What are our cost constraints? Do we have a budget we need to stay within? Do we have the time and personnel to devote to this idea?

If you answer "no" to any of these questions, it may mean that a given idea isn't realistically viable. You may need to modify your idea or move on to another option.

If you can say "yes" to all of these questions, the idea has potential. Continue to challenge it by digging in a little deeper. The following questions will help you assess whether your idea is worth the time and commitment:

- *Implementation.* Does the idea represent real value or benefit? Would others find it useful? For example, if the idea modifies an internal process within your organization, would people implement it?

- *Future opportunities.* Will the idea open the door to other opportunities or improvements?

- *Potential fallout.* If the idea doesn't work, will there be any lingering damage to the company or to team members? How easily could we recover?

Let's look at an example. Say you're trying to find a way for your organization to retain your high performers and to do so quickly. One idea on the table is to develop a new incentives-based bonus system.

You've established that this kind of system aligns with your organization's values and culture, and you have the resources and finances available to implement it. You're confident that it can easily be set up in a short time frame. Now dig deeper with your team. Here's how your thinking might play out:

Does the idea represent real value or benefit? Would others find it useful? Yes. We know that financial reward is a leading factor for retention of star performers, and it may also encourage some of our average performers to improve. That's a direct benefit to the company because we'll get better performance, and individuals will find it both useful and appealing.

Will the idea open the door to other opportunities or improvements? After we see whether there is improvement, we'll be able to consider other incentive efforts, and we can use the successful program to attract new workers.

If the idea doesn't work, will there be any lingering damage to the company or team members? How easily could we recover? If this idea doesn't work, not only will we continue to struggle with retaining our top performers, but there may also be some upset employees in the company, particularly those who become frustrated when they don't meet the requirements for a bonus. These people may also find new jobs, leaving the rest of the workers shorthanded.

Answering these questions for each of your ideas can help you and your team determine which option on your long list is the best solution. Once you've narrowed down your list to one specific path to pursue, you can then decide how to proceed.

Identify next steps

To move forward with your new idea, you and your team need a clear blueprint for how to implement it.

Begin with a detailed explanation of your proposal so you and your team members are all on the same page. Write down the idea clearly in a variety of ways—both in short form and in long form. For example, ask your team members to jot down the elevator pitch, or limit them to only one sheet of paper on which to write a brief description. Then go into more detail by outlining exactly what the team plans to do, why it will work, and why it matters. Describing your idea a few different ways will help the group crystallize the idea and unearth any lingering questions. You'll also have those explanations handy when you need to share your plan with others, whether that's a quick pitch during a hallway discussion or a longer breakdown during a planning meeting.

Next, consider what you need to move your plan toward fruition. The right way to move forward will be highly dependent on the idea you're pursuing. To help you determine this, discuss the following questions among your team:

- *Who will be involved?* Define the key stakeholders for this idea: decision makers, participants, and supporters. Whose buy-in is critical? What other individuals or departments need to take part to make this idea a success? What will each of those people need to contribute to the plan?

- *What resources are needed?* Identify where you might need specific technology, office space, or equipment. How will we get the resources we need?

- *What are the costs?* What funds are required to execute this idea? In addition, consider personnel time—training programs, operational changes, and other disruptions from the daily routine.

- *Where will the idea meet resistance?* Who might resist the idea, and why? How might we overcome opposition to the plan?

Once you've clearly outlined answers to these questions, you'll be able to prioritize what you should do and identify next steps. For example, if you discover that your project will require a large time and financial commitment—a new experimental software system that lets your customer service representatives video chat with each member of your online community—you'll first need to get buy-in from potential stakeholders and combat any resistance in order to get the funding you need. Alternatively, if your team has figured out a new way to create an informal mentorship program between experienced and new workers, you'll first need to identify where, when, and how these meetings will take place—the resources and time costs—before getting participants to take part. You can then use your answers to lay out next steps.

Finally, determine how you will measure success—how you know whether your idea worked or if you need to modify it or look for another option. For instance, if you're developing a new product, what sales numbers are you aiming for? If you're deciding how to break down silos between your design and sales departments, what kind of engagement do you want to see from your employees? If you're trying to improve employee retention rates, how will you evaluate which changes are due to your new incentive system and whether it needs to do more? Answers to these questions will help you and your team boost the odds of seeing your promising new idea become successful for your company.

With next steps in mind, you can move your idea to execution—and you've completed the creative process. But don't close yourself off to more opportunities for creativity. You can embed inventive thinking into the everyday by fostering a creative culture.

Promoting a Creative Culture

Promoting a Creative Culture

A s we've seen throughout this book, the creative process can provide your organization with inventive solutions to imminent challenges. But creativity doesn't need to be reserved for one-off situations; you can embed it into your company's daily work. In this chapter you'll learn about ways to make your organization more encouraging of innovation and creativity, from modifying the physical environment to offering support and rewards.

Enrich the physical environment

Your workplace can have more of an effect on your creative endeavors than you might imagine. Reconfiguring a meeting room for a one-time discussion is a great start. But engineering your organization's overall physical environment to encourage inventive thinking and communication can build creativity over time. A workspace that invites face-to-face interactions and chance encounters, especially one filled with many types of creative stimuli, can encourage people to make new connections and to think more broadly about problem solving and finding new opportunities.

Casual conversations and spontaneous meetings can spark innovative ideas in unexpected ways. Part of the power of these interactions—which often occur around coffee machines or water coolers and in other public areas such as copy rooms or kitchens—may be the fact that they're unplanned. Take note of the places people are already gathering informally, and make them more comfortable places to linger. Add comfortable chairs that encourage people to sit and converse. One company designed staircases wide enough for people to stop and chat. Another placed beanbag chairs in conference rooms to create a more casual atmosphere. Bring in snacks every week or two and invite your team to take a break just to talk.

Place tools for creativity and communication in unexpected places. Some organizations leave whiteboards, markers, and flip charts in informal meeting spaces—in the kitchen, for example. These tools inspire people to capture and sketch out ideas during a spontaneous discussion. Other companies distribute crayons and white paper on conference room tables to encourage doodling and making diagrams, enabling a mode of thought that's different from the usual verbal discussion.

Find opportunities for play using games and other stress relievers. Play serves a serious function: When employees are clattering a ball around a foosball table, they may also be subconsciously unwinding a sticky work problem. Giving the conscious mind a break from the problem at hand allows a person to later return to work refreshed—perhaps with a new approach or a unique solution.

Keep in mind, though, that as with your diverse team, your organization has many different ways of working and thinking. Beyond these open, collaborative spaces, create areas for quiet work and reflection: a company library where silence is expected or meeting rooms where doors can shut out distractions.

Encourage risk and learning

In addition to considering your company's physical environment, look at its psychological setting. Creative problem solving and inventive thinking will only flourish in an organization that welcomes them.

Innovation should be viewed as a normal part of business.

Encourage individuals within your company to take risks. Innovative progress and risk are inseparable. One new idea could easily fail, but another could have great benefits. An organization that recognizes this dynamic must communicate that reasonable risks aren't only acceptable, they're necessary to keep the company moving forward.

Encourage knowledge sharing across the organization. Tightly controlling information limits the opportunity for knowledge to combine and intersect in ways that can spur innovation and creative thinking. Make opportunities for your employees to share information and bring new ideas to the fore. Encourage communities of interest, groups of people across the organization with similar passions, to communicate and exchange ideas. Urge employees to gain insight from external sources by attending professional meetings and conferences, visiting customers, and meeting experts. The more knowledge that's exchanged and brought into your organization, the more likely it is to be used in creative ways.

Establish a reward system

Inspire idea champions. Network with influential people within your organization, and make sure they take notice of especially creative efforts. Attention from organizational leadership signals to an individual, a team, and the rest of the company that a project is important. And that attention can be a powerful motivator for continued creative work. Executives who stand behind good ideas can provide not only moral support but also protection and resources to new endeavors. Such support—and the rewards that come with it—can further motivate employees to bring their creative ideas to life.

Most people naturally associate the word "reward" with money or bonuses. Such extrinsic rewards—

which include additional pay, a vacation, or even special recognition—appeal to a person's desire to attain a goal that is distinct from the work itself. But these external awards aren't the only way to motivate your employees to continue their inventive efforts. Intrinsic rewards can appeal to a person's desire for self-actualization or challenge, to her deep interest and involvement in the work, or to her curiosity or sense of enjoyment.

Four types of intrinsic and extrinsic rewards can support and encourage your employees to continue their inventive efforts:

- *Recognition.* A sense of making progress is a powerful motivator. Publicly acknowledge an individual or group with an announcement or award. For example, ask a high-level executive to share her appreciation for what a team is doing. Or publicly recognize a person who has worked outside his preferred style or function.

- *Control.* Involve an individual or group in making a decision or choice that affects them. Grant them the autonomy to solve problems on their own. For example, after a successful customer engagement event, invite your team members to choose a new marketing opportunity to think about next. Or give them increasingly challenging projects to tackle that pique their interests.

- *Celebration.* Applaud a successful venture by throwing a small party. Toast a new product's launch, or take your employees out to dinner after successfully launching a redesigned website.

- *Rejuvenation.* Offer time off or time away from a given task. Give team members extra vacation days for breaking your company's core cereal brand into a new international market. Or send individuals to industry conferences so they can develop their skills, build relationships, and come back to work renewed and energized.

You can stimulate *and* sustain your team's creative energy—and help people make progress every day—with a thoughtfully constructed system of rewards and support in an atmosphere of openness. Building a culture that maximizes creative momentum can help you lead your team through the process of generating and implementing new solutions to the tough challenges you face.

Creativity can provide your organization with fresh thinking and exciting solutions to anything from everyday problems to big challenges. Don't leave this kind of inventive thinking to the "creatives" in your organization: Empower your whole team to generate and act on great ideas.

Learn More

Quick Hits

"Designing Spaces for Creative Collaboration." HBR.org Idea-cast, January 19, 2012. https://hbr.org/2012/01/designing-spaces-for-creative/.

In this interview, Scott Doorley and Scott Witthoft of Stanford University's Institute of Design, or "d.school," discuss how to design your organization's physical space to enhance creative potential. They suggest small but significant changes that can promote an inventive and collaborative culture—from choosing chairs that promote active engagement to putting visual work on display to creating pop-up meeting spaces.

Kelley, Tom and David Kelley. "Three Creativity Challenges from IDEO's Leaders." HBR.org. November 8, 2013. https://hbr.org/2013/11/three-creativity-challenges-from-ideos-leaders/.

Creativity takes practice, argue IDEO's Tom Kelley and David Kelley, and the more you do it, the easier it gets. In this piece, the authors provide diagrams and step-by-step instructions for three exercises to help readers improve their creative skills both individually and as a team.

Richardson, Adam. "Boosting Creativity Through Constraints." HBR.org, June 11, 2013. https://hbr.org/2013/06/boosting-creativity-through-co.

Conventional wisdom says that the best way to boost a team's creativity is to release participants from all constraints. But it turns out that some restrictions can help your team find clarity of purpose in its creative efforts. In this piece, Richardson helps readers understand when a constraint can enhance creativity and when it needs to be removed or replaced.

Books

Harvard Business Essentials: The Innovator's Toolkit. Boston: Harvard Business Press, 2009.

How can you generate creative ideas for your business? How can you translate ideas into an actual innovative product or service? This book provides techniques and practical tips to show readers how to develop and implement innovative ideas, from generating ideas to testing the business potential of options to moving an innovation forward with a strategic plan.

Leonard, Dorothy and Walter Swap. *When Sparks Fly: Igniting Creativity in Groups.* Boston: Harvard Business School Publishing, 1999.

Most innovations come from well-led group interactions, say organizational behavior experts Leonard and Swap. This book digs deeply into the creative process, explaining how to effectively design and manage a creative team to produce more-innovative services, products, and processes. Managers will discover how to influence all aspects of the work environment—from leadership style to motivation to the use of space—to enhance creativity and innovation.

Thompson, Leigh. *Creative Conspiracy: The New Rules of Breakthrough Collaboration*. Boston: Harvard Business Review Press, 2013.

According to management expert Thompson, collaboration that is conscious, planned, and focused on generating new ideas builds excitement and produces a "creative conspiracy." In this book, readers will learn how to help their teams reach their full creative potential and maximize their results by creating a diverse and social team, facilitating and motivating group collaboration, improving brainstorming's effectiveness, transforming conflict into creativity, and more.

Articles

Amabile, Teresa M., Constance N. Hadley, and Steven J. Kramer. "Creativity Under the Gun." *Harvard Business Review*, August 2002 (product #R0208C).

Does working under a tight deadline enhance your creative efforts? While in most instances the answer is no, sometimes these situations are unavoidable. In this piece, the authors provide readers with a variety of tips and advice based on research to soften the negative effects of time pressure, from shielding your team members from distractions to helping them discover the importance of their efforts.

Catmull, Ed. "How Pixar Fosters Collective Creativity." *Harvard Business Review*, September 2008 (product #R0809D).

In this article, the president of Pixar and Disney Animation Studios explains how to build a sustainable creative organization. Using Pixar as an example, Catmull shares the principles the company uses to create successful films. By studying the case, readers will learn how to take risks, lead a creative vision, promote a supportive culture, and overcome bumps in the road.

Saunders, Rebecca M. "Better Brainstorming." *Harvard Management Communication Letter*, November 1999 (product #C9911C).

Brainstorming may be a familiar technique for generating ideas, but it's not always as effective as it could be. In this article, experts share a number of ways to keep ideas flowing and make brainstorming sessions more productive—in both quantity and quality. Tips include defining the problem as a group, inviting innovative thinkers to your meeting, adding physical activity to your idea generation session, and using "assumption reversals" to look at problems in new ways.

Sources

Amabile, Teresa M. "Creativity and Innovation in Organizations." Case note N9-396-239. Boston: Harvard Business School, 1996 (product #396239)

———. "How to Kill Creativity." *Harvard Business Review*, September 1998 (product #98501).

Amabile, Teresa M., Constance N. Hadley, and Steven J. Kramer. "Creativity Under the Gun." *Harvard Business Review*, August 2002 (product #R0208C).

Amabile, Teresa M. and Mukti Khaire. "Creativity and the Role of the Leader." *Harvard Business Review*, October 2008 (product #R0810G).

Amabile, Teresa M. and Steven J. Kramer. "The Power of Small Wins." *Harvard Business Review*, May 2011 (product #R1105C).

Anthony, Scott D. "My Simplest Innovation Advice." HBR.org, February 25, 2011. https://hbr.org/2011/02/my-simplest-innovation-advice/.

———. *The Little Black Book of Innovation*. Boston: Harvard Business Review Press, 2012.

Barrett, Derm. *The Paradox Process*. New York: AMACOM, 1997.

Cannon, Mark and Amy Edmondson. "Confronting Failure: Antecedents and Consequences of Shared Beliefs About Failure in Organizational Work Groups." Special Issue on Shared Cognition. *Journal of Organizational Behavior* 22, no. 2 (March 2001).

Coyne, Kevin P., Patricia Gorman Clifford, and Renée Dye. "Breakthrough Thinking from Inside the Box." *Harvard Business Review*, December 2007 (product #R0712E).

Csikszentmihalyi, Mihaly. *Creativity: Flow and the Psychology of Discovery and Invention.* New York: HarperCollins, 1996.

Drucker, Peter. "The Discipline of Innovation." *Harvard Business Review*, August 2002 (product #R0208F).

Duarte, Nancy. "Create a Presentation Your Audience Will Care About." HBR.org. October 10, 2012. https://hbr.org/2012/10/create-presentations-an-audien/.

———. *HBR Guide to Persuasive Presentations.* Boston: Harvard Business Review Press, 2012.

Florida, Richard and Jim Goodnight. "Managing for Creativity." *Harvard Business Review*, July 2005 (product #R0507L).

Gilbert, Julie. "How to Lead Better Brainstorming Sessions." HBR.org, May 4, 2009. https://hbr.org/2009/05/how-to-lead-better-brainstormi/.

Govindarajan, Vijay. "Innovation Is Not Creativity." HBR.org, August 3, 2010. https://hbr.org/2010/08/innovation-is-not-creativity/.

Govindarajan, Vijay and Srikanth Srinivas. "The Right Innovation Mindset Can Take You from Idea to Impact." HBR.org, September 19, 2013. https://hbr.org/2013/09/the-right-innovation-mindset-can-take-you-from-idea-to-impact/.

Harvard Business School Publishing. *Harvard Business Essentials: Decision Making: 5 Steps to Better Results*. Boston: Harvard Business School Publishing, 2006.

———. *Harvard Business Essentials: The Innovator's Toolkit*. Boston: Harvard Business Press, 2009.

———. *Harvard Business Essentials: Managing Creativity and Innovation*. Boston: Harvard Business School Publishing, 2003.

———. "Innovation and Creativity," Harvard ManageMentor. Boston: Harvard Business School Publishing, 2010.

———. *Pocket Mentor: Fostering Creativity*. Boston: Harvard Business Press, 2010.

———. *Running Meetings* (20-Minute Manager series). Boston: Harvard Business Review Press, 2014.

———. "Strategic Thinking," Harvard ManageMentor. Boston: Harvard Business School Publishing, 2010.

Hill, Linda A. "Becoming the Boss." *Harvard Business Review*, January 2007 (product #R0701D).

Hill, Linda A., Greg Brandeau, Emily Truelove, and Kent Lineback. *Collective Genius*. Boston: Harvard Business Review Press, 2014.

Isaksen, Scott G., K. Brian Dorval, and Donald J. Treffinger. *Creative Approaches to Problem Solving*. Dubuque, IA: Kendall/Hunt Publishing Company, 1994.

———. *Toolbox for Creative Problem Solving*. Williamsville, NY: Creative Problem Solving Group, 1998.

Kelley, Tom, and David Kelley. "Reclaim Your Creative Confidence." *Harvard Business Review*, December 2012 (product #R1212K).

Kirby, Julia. "Are We Being Creative Yet?" *Harvard Business Review*, March 2012.

Leonard, Dorothy. *Managing Groups for Creativity and Innovation*. Boston: Harvard Business School Publishing, 1998.

Leonard, Dorothy and Walter Swap. *When Sparks Fly: Harnessing the Power of Group Creativity*. Boston: Harvard Business School Publishing, 1999.

Michalko, Michael. *Cracking Creativity: The Secrets of Creative Genius*. Berkeley, CA: Ten Speed Press, 1998.

Miller, William C. *Flash of Brilliance*. Reading, MA: Perseus Books, 1999.

"Mind Mapping." *Harvard Management Communication Letter*, November 2000 (product #C0011E).

Nussbaum, Bruce. "How to Find and Amplify Creativity." HBR.org. March 7, 2013. https://hbr.org/2013/03/how-to-find-and-amplify-creati/.

Pallotta, Dan. "What's the Point of Creativity?" HBR.org. September 9, 2013. https://hbr.org/2013/09/does-your-innovation-come-from/.

Richardson, Adam. "Inventing the Collaborative Workspace." HBR.org, November 21, 2011. https://hbr.org/2011/11/inventing-the-collaborative-workspace/.

Robinson, Alan G. and Sam Stern. *Corporate Creativity*. San Francisco: Berrett-Koehler, 1997.

Saunders, Rebecca M. "Better Brainstorming." *Harvard Management Communication Letter*, November 1999 (product #C9911C).

Sethi, Rajesh, Daniel C. Smith, and C. Whan Park. "How to Kill a Team's Creativity." *Harvard Business Review*, August 2002 (product #F0208B).

Shapiro, Mary. *HBR Guide to Leading Teams*. Boston: Harvard Business Review Press, 2014.

"Sparking Creativity at Ferrari: A Conversation with Mario Almondo." *Harvard Business Review*, April 2006 (product #F0604F).

Thompson, Leigh. *Creative Conspiracy: The New Rules of Breakthrough Collaboration*. Boston: Harvard Business Review Press, 2013.

"The Truth About Creative Teams." HBR.org Ideacast, April 4, 2013. https://hbr.org/2013/04/the-truth-about-creative-teams/.

Waber, Ben, Jennifer Magnolfi, and Greg Lindsay. "Workspaces That Move People." *Harvard Business Review*, October 2014 (product #R1410E).

Witthoft, Scott and Scott Doorley. "Five Ways to Make Corporate Space More Creative." HBR.org, March 28, 2012. https://hbr.org/2012/03/five-ways-to-make-corporate-sp/.

Zelinski, Ernie J. *The Joy of Thinking Big*. Berkeley, CA: Ten Speed Press, 1998.

Index

Notes

Notes

Notes

Notes

Notes